SOLO Wildlife

Lion

Written and illustrated
by David Kennett

SOLOS

For Harry

Southwood Books Limited
4 Southwood Lawn Road
London N6 5SF

First published in Australia by Omnibus Books 2001
This edition published in the UK under licence from
Omnibus Books by
Southwood Books Limited, 2001.

Text and illustrations copyright © David Kennett 2001
Cover design by Lyn Mitchell
Typeset by Clinton Ellicott, Adelaide
Printed in Singapore

ISBN 1 903207 41 X

The lion

is a warm-blooded animal

lives in a family group or pride – the females hunt and the males protect pride members and their territory

has long been killed by humans as a test of the hunter's skill and bravery

is a protected animal in many parts of Africa.

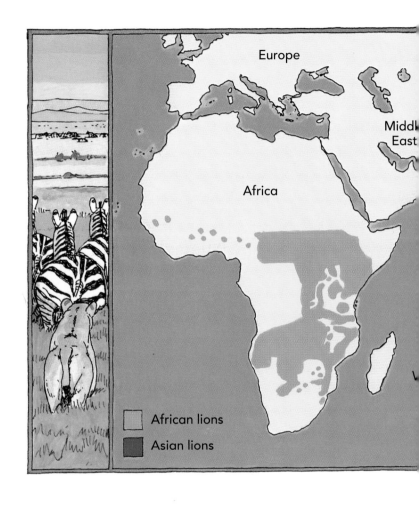

Many years ago lions lived in Africa, the Middle East, India, and southern Europe. Today you will find wild lions only in Africa and India.

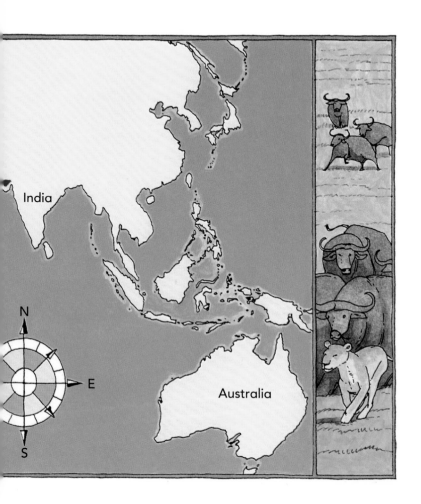

The small number of lions in India live in a forest reserve. This map shows where lions live now.

The lion is one of the biggest of the world's wild cats.

The maps show where each animal lives.

Lion

Leopard

Snow leopard

0   1   2

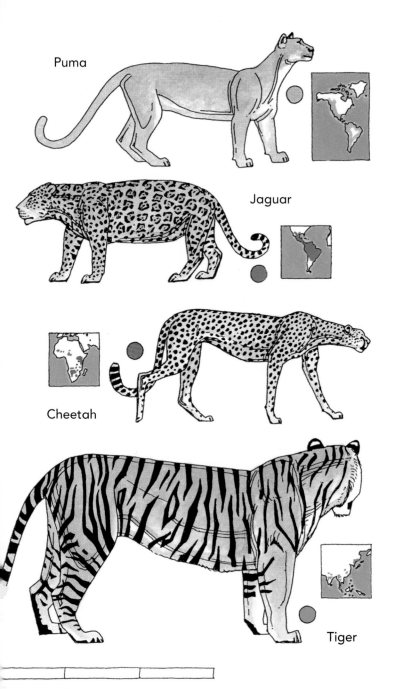

Puma

Jaguar

Cheetah

Tiger

3　　　　4 metres　　　　5

Like people, some lions are bigger than others. This lion measures 220 centimetres from the base of its tail to its nose. It is 120 centimetres from the top of its shoulder to the ground.

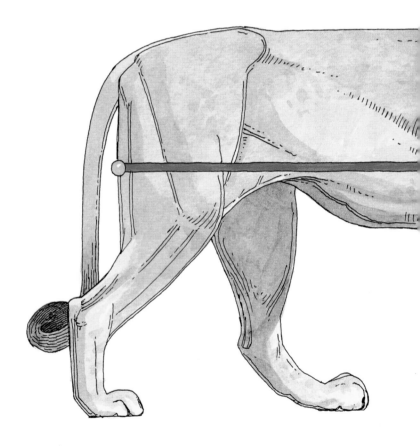

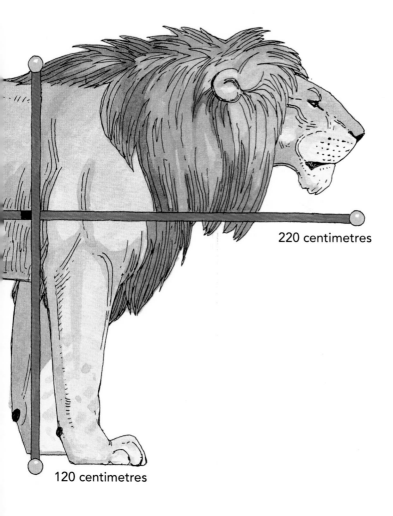

220 centimetres

120 centimetres

An African lion can weigh between 150 and 250 kilograms. This lion weighs 170 kilograms. A house cat weighs about three and a half kilograms. It would take 48 and a half cats to make up the weight of this lion.

The heaviest lion ever recorded weighed 313 kilograms.

The female lion is called a lioness.
She is smaller than the male.

An African lioness can weigh between
120 and 182 kilograms.

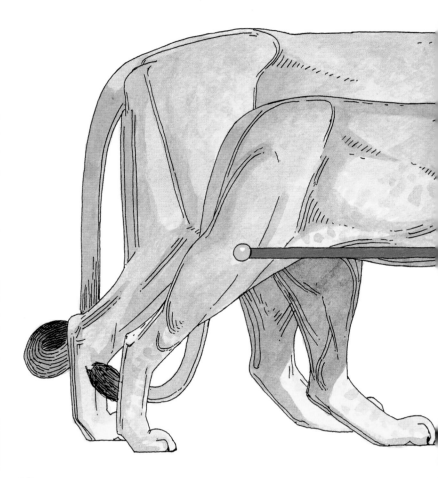

This lioness measures 160 centimetres from the base of her tail to her nose. She is 105 centimetres tall, measured from the top of her shoulder to the ground.

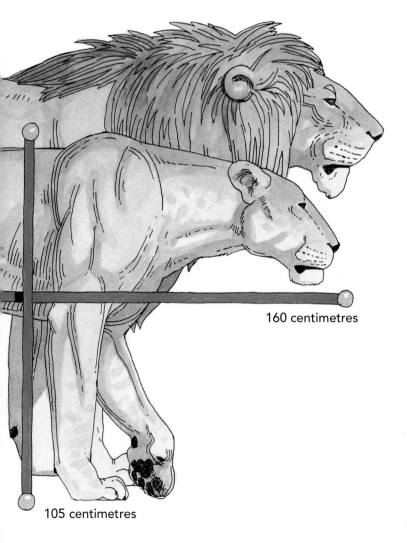

160 centimetres

105 centimetres

In the wild a lioness can live to between 15 and 20 years. A lion's life is usually shorter. He can live to about 12 years old.

A group of lions, lionesses and cubs living together is called a pride.

A pride can be big or small, but an average pride will have 15 animals.

The lionesses in a pride are usually related and will have known each other from birth. Pride members get along very well. They will lick and rub up against each other and rest close together.

Because of this contact, pride members share a similar scent. They have their own pride smell. This helps them to recognise each other.

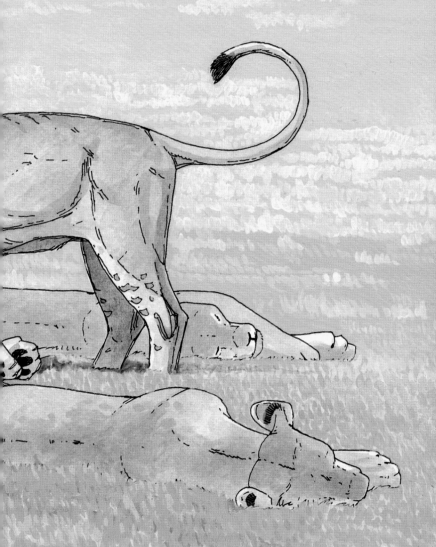

Lions stay with their pride as long as they can. One day other lions will chase them away and take over the pride.

Groups of lions compete with other
lions for a pride. There are fights, and
some lions are killed. An angry lion will
lash his tail and turn the backs of his
ears forward. A lion defending himself
will flatten his ears.

Each pride has its own territory that it defends against other lions. Where there is plenty of food the territory might be as small as 20 square kilometres. If food is scarce, it might be as big as 400 square kilometres.

The pride's scent marks its territory. Lions know the best places in their territory to hunt. They also know where to hide their cubs to keep them safe.

Lions hunt and kill animals that eat
plants. Animals that eat plants are
called herbivores.

Lions usually hunt in groups, but they
will also hunt alone.

The lionesses do most of the hunting. The lion's mane makes him easier to see. A lioness will catch more prey if he is not there. The lion will always claim his share of the food.

Hunting large prey is difficult. It is also dangerous. Lionesses can be hurt or even killed. They might catch an animal only once in every five times they hunt.

An easy meal is always welcome.
Lions will feed on animals that are
already dead. They will also steal food
from other predators.

Lions catch prey of all sizes. Their main food is medium-sized animals like zebras and wildebeest.

One pride living on the coast of Africa hunted seals for its food.

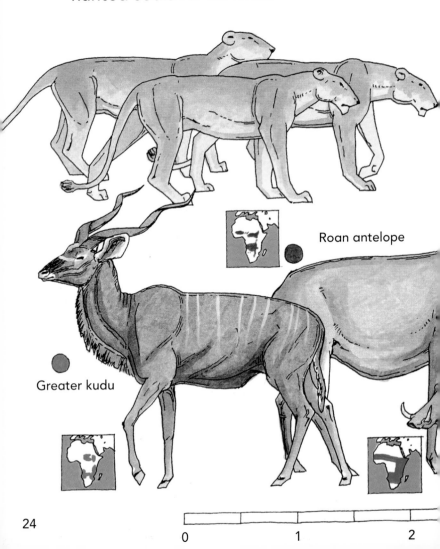

Roan antelope

Greater kudu

0   1   2

Cape buffalo

Impala

Brindled wildebeest

Warthog

Zebra

5 metres

3　　　　4

Lions are active after sunset. They often hunt at night.

When lions in a pride feed there is no set order for which one eats first. There is often a struggle over the food.

Lions do not chew their food. They swallow it in large pieces.

Lions need between five and 10 kilograms of meat every day. A lion can eat 40 kilograms of meat at one meal if he is very hungry.

Lions have thick pads on the soles of their feet. The pads stop the lion's bones from jarring when it is running or jumping.

When they are stalking their prey, lionesses need to walk quietly. The pads on their feet soften the sound of their footsteps.

Lions have four claws on their back feet and five claws on their front feet. The claws are pulled in when they are not in use. This keeps them off the ground, and so they stay sharp.

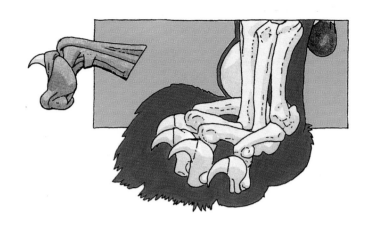

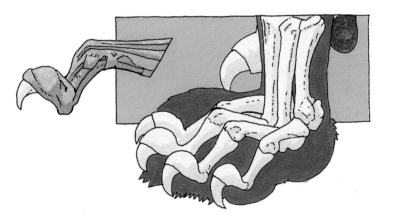

Lions use their claws to grip their prey or as weapons for fighting. They also use them as a comb for grooming.

On a pair of scissors the place that gives the most powerful bite is closest to the hinge.

Tin snips have short jaws. They can cut metal.

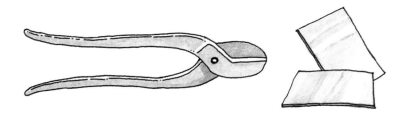

Dress making scissors have long jaws. They cut cloth.

A lion's jaws are short. This gives the lion a powerful bite.

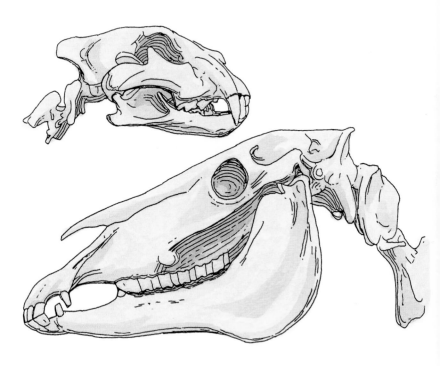

A horse's jaws are long so that they can cut and chew grass. The grinding teeth are in the back of the jaw.

Lions have 30 teeth, 15 on each side of the skull. Lions use their teeth mainly for slicing flesh.

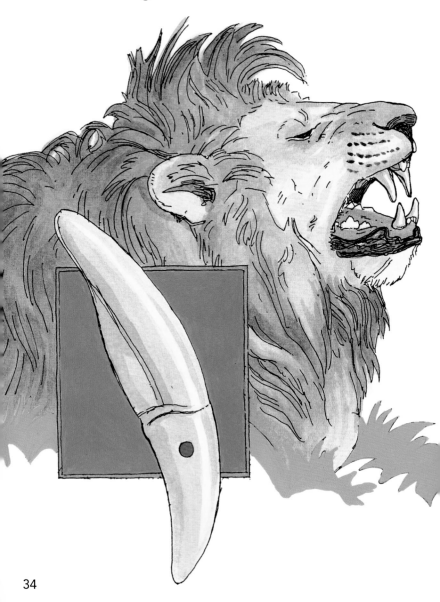

The lion's large carnassial teeth cut flesh like scissors. Their long canine teeth hold and kill prey.

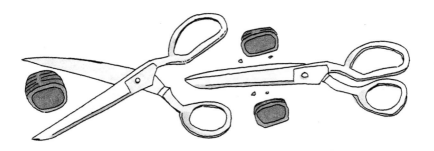

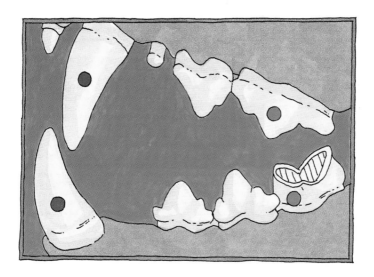

● Canine tooth

● Carnassial tooth

A lion's tongue is so rough it can scrape the meat off bones.

Lions see more clearly at night than humans do. They can also see for a longer distance.

Lions are lazy, like house cats. They rest and sleep for up to 19 hours of every day. They are active for the other five hours of the day. This is usually between sunset and sunrise.

Lions roar to find their pride or to find out where other lions are. The pride roars to proclaim its territory and to strengthen the bonds between its members.

The lions in a pride are the fathers of all the cubs in their pride. Lions start mating when they are between the ages of three and four years.

A lion and a lioness will stay together
for three or four days, mating often.

Cubs are born three and a half months after the lioness becomes pregnant. When it is time, the lioness leaves her pride and gives birth to her cubs in a hidden spot.

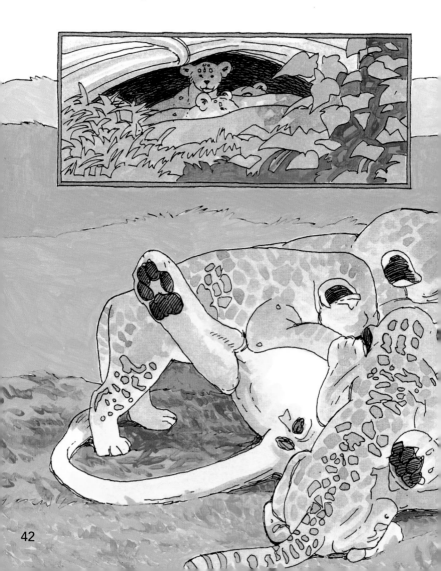

She usually has two to four cubs.
When cubs are born they weigh about
1.36 kilograms. They are helpless.
Their eyes are closed at first. They
open their eyes 10 to 14 days after
they are born.

Newborn cubs are in constant danger. Their mother has to leave them when she goes hunting. Hyenas, leopards, jackals or other lions might find and kill them.

The mother moves her new cubs by carrying them gently in her mouth, just as a house cat does.

Only about a half of the cubs that are born will become adults.

Lions in the pride may have the chance to mate only once. They have as many cubs as they can at the one time. They may not be with the pride long enough to defend their cubs.

The lionesses in a pride will often have
their cubs at around the same time.
The mothers feed and protect all the
cubs in the pride.

When cubs are 18 months old they are called sub-adults. At about this age the cubs' fathers are often chased away by a new group of lions.

The sub-adult males are also chased off. The sub-adult females often stay with the pride.

Lions that have just taken over a pride will kill the cubs. They do this so that they can mate with the lionesses and have their own cubs. They are in a hurry, because other lions will take over the pride if they can.

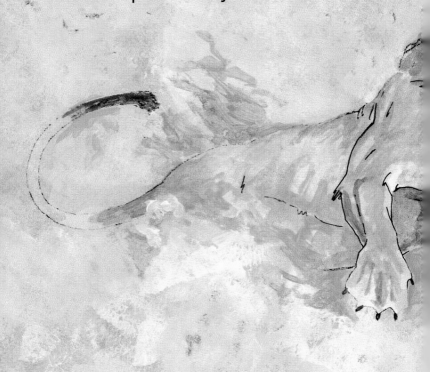

Male lions have to defend the pride's territory. They also have to mark the territory with their scent and urine and fight off strange lions.

The lion's mane protects his neck
during fights. The mane changes to a
darker colour as he grows older. It may
even turn black.

In the ancient Roman world lions were made to fight other animals and to kill people. These shows were held in arenas. The most famous arena is the Colosseum in Rome.

The lion has always been admired as
a brave and strong animal. Knights
from long ago used a picture of the
lion to show they were brave fighters.

The ancient Egyptians believed in many gods. One of these was called Sekhmet. She had the head of a lion and was goddess of war.

The sphinx is a large statue of a lion with the head of a man. It was built a long time ago in Egypt.

According to Greek legend the sun god
Apollo created the lion. His twin sister,
the moon goddess Artemis, created
the house cat to make fun of him.

The ancient Greek hero Herakles killed the Nemean lion and wore its skin.

The lion is a protected animal in some African countries.

The biggest threat to lions is always going to be the loss of land for them to live on.

For the present some countries have areas where lions can live wild. Tourists spend money to come and see them.

Glossary

arena • place where games are held, with seats for people to watch.

carnivore • animal that eats meat as its main food.

herbivore • animal that eats plants as its main food.

grooming • cleaning and combing the fur.

mane • the long hair on a lion's neck.

Nemean lion • the lion of Nemea, which Herakles had to kill as one of his labours, in the old Greek story.

predator • animal that hunts and kills other animals for its food.

prey • an animal that is hunted and killed by another animal.

pride • family group of lions.

proclaim • let others know something.

protected animal • an animal that people are not allowed to hunt or kill.

scent • an animal's own smell.

stalking • creeping up on prey.

sub-adult • animal that is not yet an adult.

territory • the area of land that an animal hunts in and defends against other animals.

warm-blooded animal • an animal whose blood temperature stays at between 36 and 44 degrees Celsius in cold or hot weather. Humans keep their temperature at this level in winter by wearing warm clothes.

Index